I KNOW WHO I AM

The ABC's of Positive Self-Affirmations for Children

Portia Smith

Published by:
Imagine Me, Creative Book Publishing an Imprint of Perfectly Payten, LLC

Library of Congress Control Number:
2020910391

DEDICATION

To my loving and amazing children,
Mark and Payten, who inspire me daily to keep
going and to remain strong.

Love Mom.

ACKNOWLEDGMENTS

Thank you to my mother, father, brother, sister, children, and friends for patiently giving me advice, love, and encouragement while completing this book. Special thanks to Paige and Tiffany for being a listening ear and decision makers! You guys rock!

Look in the mirror and tell me what do you see.
Mommy, I see someone wonderful looking back at me.
I see an amazing, marvelous, incredible me!

You are indeed a special child, always humble, meek, and mild. Positive thinking is a powerful tool. Through the alphabets, we can learn that positive self-affirmations are cool.
So, children come along, let's take a look.
We can read affirmations like a book.

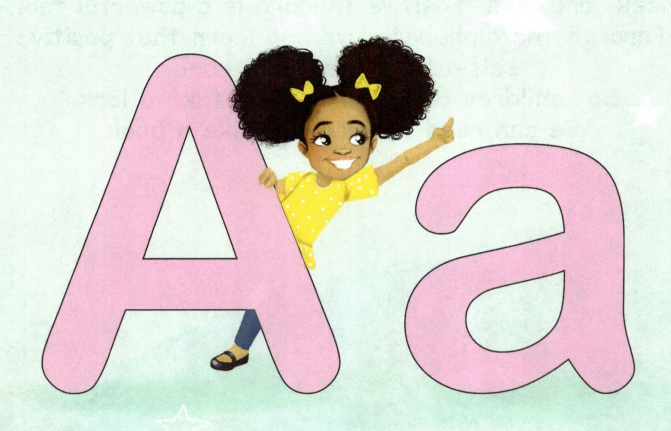

I am AWESOME!

I am BRAVE!

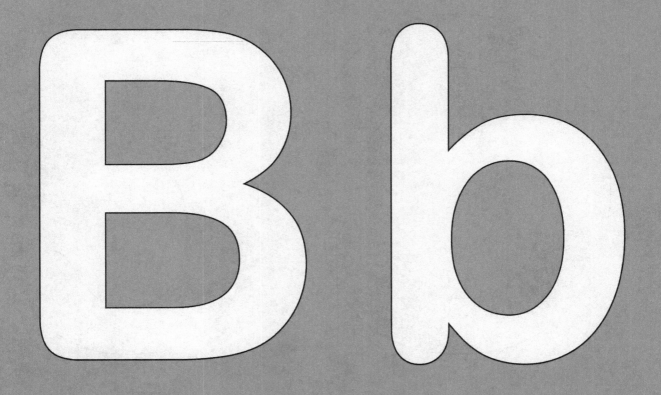

I am CARING!

I am DEPENDABLE!

E e

I am ENERGETIC!

I am FRIENDLY!

Ff

Gg

I am GRATEFUL!

I am HAPPY!

Hh

I am IMPORTANT!

I am JOYFUL!

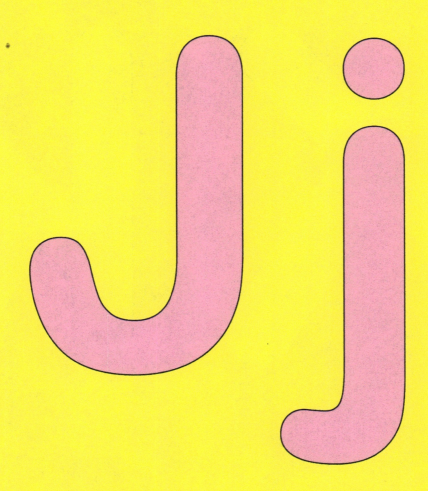

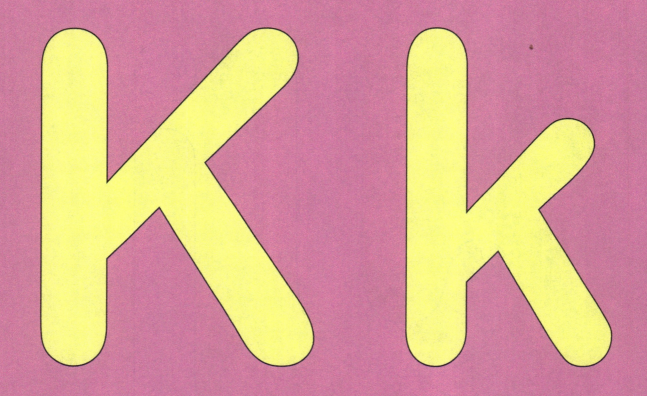

I am KIND!

I am LOVED!

I am MAGNIFICENT!

I am NICE!

I am OUTSTANDING!

I am PROUD!

Pp

I am QUALIFIED!

I am RESPECTFUL!

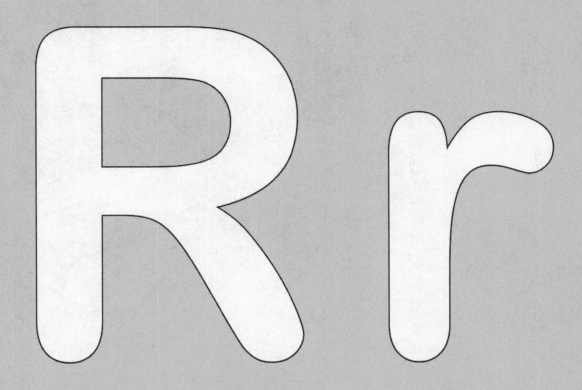

I am STRONG!

I am THOUGHTFUL!

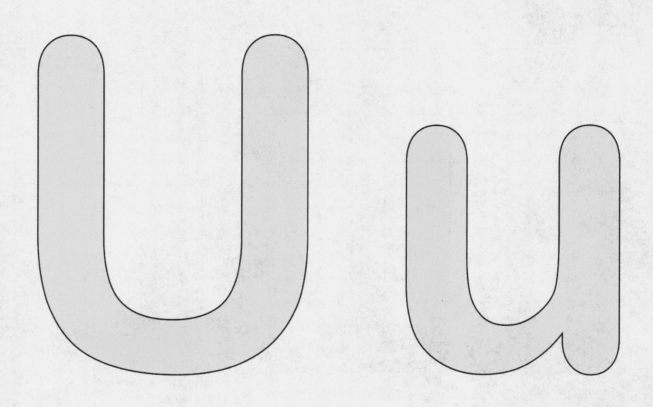

I am UNIQUE!

I am VALUABLE!

V v

I am WONDERFUL!

I am XENIAL!

I am
YOUTHFUL!

I am ZESTFUL!

Zz

I learned that
I am awesome, brave,
and as strong as I can be.
I learned that
I am somebody
and I can empower me.

ABOUT THE AUTHOR

Portia Smith is a Licensed Professional Counselor, Certified Professional Counselor Supervisor, and a Certified Rehabilitation Counselor. She has over ten years of both clinical and professional experience in the mental health field. She specializes in suicide and crisis intervention, and prevention services. She is a huge advocate for self-care and mental health wellness. She strives to enhance confidence and positive selfesteem in others.

Portia is a loving and devoted mother of two. In her spare time, she enjoys arts and crafts. Portia also loves working within her community and is a dedicated member of the Alpha Kappa Alpha Sorority, Incorporated.

CPSIA information can be obtained
at www.ICGtesting.com
Printed in the USA
LVHW061113190720
661079LV00004B/325